Make a Memory
Every Day

Make a Memory Every Day

Vol. 1

GOD'S WORD WILL CHANGE YOUR LIFE

JERILYN PALLESI VON FLUE

XULON PRESS

Xulon Press
2301 Lucien Way #415
Maitland, FL 32751
407.339.4217
www.xulonpress.com

Paperback ISBN-13: 978-1-66285-738-6
Ebook ISBN-13: 978-1-66285-739-3

Memories

Memories are made of things
That happen every day
Moments as we live them
Things we do or say

Little bits and pieces
Of laughter mixed with tears
Paragraphs and pages
Written through the years

The Friendships we remember
Mistakes that we regret
The ending of a love
We never could forget

We can't erase the sadness
Or edit out the tears
We can't undo the wrongs
We can't relive the years

But since memories keep building
Each day can be the start
Of making new and happy ones
To store within the heart.

-Jerilyn Pallesi Von Flue

Dedication

I'd like to dedicate this book to these wonderful ladies who have been a part of my life.

Fern Pallesi (MOM): A Beautiful example of a prayer warrior and the discipline of being in God's Word every day. If I needed someone to pray for me, pray for one of my friends, my children or just anything, I could always call and ask her to pray. I knew beyond a shadow of a doubt, she would drop everything she was doing at that moment and begin to pray. I can't begin to explain the feeling of knowing when you ask someone to pray that they touch the throne room of heaven with their prayers. 1 Peter 3:12a NIV "For the eyes of the Lord are on the righteous and his ears are attentive to their prayer" .... I want to leave a legacy like that for my children and their children and their children's children.

Evelyn Annis (Aunt): She invited me to a Women's Bible Study at her church and the woman who was teaching told the story about her and a friend challenging each other by memorizing chapters of the book of Psalms every day. They would call each other and recite the verses that they had memorized. I felt God speaking to me then, you'll be doing that someday....... Thank you Aunt Evelyn so much for inviting me, that planted a seed that's been growing in me for years and has never been forgotten.

Kathren Shuey (Sunday School Teacher): From a very young age I had a gift for memorization. I loved spelling and aced my spelling test every week in school. My mom and dad were faithful to take me to Sunday School and church every week. I couldn't wait to be in Kathren Shuey's Sunday School class. She had 2 grade levels, 4th and 5th graders. I remember watching the kids coming out of her class with prizes and candy. To this day I can still see the flower printed canvas suitcase that she carried all those well-earned treasures for the children. I didn't realize what a profound impact she was going to have on my life. It amazes me what a few prizes and sweet treats can do to encourage a child to memorize scripture. That was a pivotal moment in my life and I know one day in heaven, I will see her face to face and thank her for being obedient to serve as my Sunday School Teacher and OF COURSE, the prizes and treats.

Dorothy Lutz (English Teacher): She was a positive person and encouraged her students to express themselves and write from their hearts. It was my senior year and I had a writing assignment that was due in her class and I had turned mine in early. I'll never forget that day when she pulled me aside at her desk and said "Jerilyn, you have a real gift for writing that you should pursue." I've never forgotten the elated feeling....I could really do it and she was proud of me. Since that time if I have seen a special ability or talent in someone, I make sure to tell them. WORDS ARE POWERFUL! A seed of confidence was also planted in my life that day from just a few words from a beautiful lady and Friend.

Attitude of Gratitude

I have so many people in my life I have to be thankful for, all have inspired me in one way or another. I have my parents to thank who were faithful to take me to Sunday School, learning the Word of God which allowed me to plant it deep in my heart. I'm thankful for all of my Sunday School teachers who every week sacrificed their time but also to those of you out there who are doing the same. You may never know how much of an influence you have made in a Child's life until you get to Heaven. I love my job and bosses that I have had and now have that challenge me everyday to do "exceeding and abundantly" more than I ever thought I could do, stretching and growing me every minute. I love my husband and I thank God for him, he puts up with my silliness and quirky personality, never knowing what plans I have for him to do. Next up "My Children", who I dearly love. My Sons, Andrew and Nicholas, who have grown into wonderful Young Men and my beautiful daughter Arielle. I also have 2 daughter-in-laws, Amber and Megeanne and hopefully a son-in-law someday. *"Grandchildren are the crowning glory of the aged; parents are the pride of their children." Proverbs 17:6 NLT.* I think this verse says it all about our 8 grandchildren, and our "Children", did you notice, it states "PARENTS are the Pride of their Children". Hum!!! Imagine that! To My Sister, Diane who has always loved me. From the day I was born, I was her "Real Live Baby Doll". She encourages me everyday and lifts me up when needed, and she's also a wonderful cook that inspires me to try new things. I'm thankful for my Brother-in-law, Ken, always assisting us with our yard and in turn, I order him online Ice Cream delivered to his doorstep..."fair trade" as he would say. I'm fortunate to have wonderful family and friends who have encouraged, inspired and prayed for me along the way, too many to list and I wouldn't want to forget anyone, but you know who you are. Cousins, Bill and Karen Slentz, Bill is a Children's Book Illustrator, Writer and Publisher of Eleven "Arnold A. Airplane" books and "The Great American Cross-Country Flying Excursion" and Karen is his Biggest Cheerleader. Bill gave me a "Yes" when I asked if I should publish a book. That was the assuring word that this was what God wanted me to do. Last but not least, thank you to my cousin, Shelley Stinnett who spent hours reviewing and rereading this book for content, suggestions and accuracy. All I can say is a "BIG" Thank You!

Make a Memory Every Day

During this Memory Devotion book, I want to challenge you to memorize scripture. Whether you read the book through or take one Memory at a time, let the word of God penetrate your Mind, Soul and Spirit. These are just a few of my favorite scriptures, not in any particular order, except the 1st one. There are 2 ways to read this book, either like a daily devotion or just read it like a good book that you can't put down. If you do that, then go back and memorize, memorize and memorize. Allow the Word of God to sink deep into your spirit. Happy Reading and Memorizing!

> *"I have hidden your word in my heart that I might not sin against you." Psalms 119:11 NIV*

> *"For God has not given us a spirit of fear, but of power and of love and of a sound mind." 2 Timothy 1:7 NKJV*

> *"The tongue has the power of life and death, and those who love it will eat its fruit." Proverbs 18:21 NIV*

> *"I can do all things through Christ who strengthens me" Philippians 4:13 NKJV*

> *"Be anxious for nothing but in everything by prayer and supplication, with thanksgiving, let your requests be made known to God; and the peace*

of God which surpasses all understanding, will guard your hearts and minds through Christ Jesus." *Philippians 4:6-7 NKJV*

" Merry Heart does good like a medicine, but a Broken Spirit dries up the bones." *Proverbs 17:22 NKJV*

"So do not fear, for I am with you; do not be dismayed, for I am your God. I will strengthen you and help you; I will uphold you with my righteous right hand." *Isaiah 41:10 NIV*

"If my people, who are called by my name, will humble themselves and pray and seek my face and turn from their wicked ways, then I will hear from heaven, and I will forgive their sin and will heal their land. Now my eyes will be open and my ears attentive to the prayers offered in this place." *II Chronicles 7:14-15 NIV*

"The Lord will fight for you, you need only to be still." *Exodus 14:14 NIVz*

He says, "Be still, and know that I am God; I will be exalted among the nations, I will be exalted in the earth." *Psalms 46:10 NIV*

Jesus looked at them and said, "With man this is impossible, but with God all things are possible." *Matthew 19:26 NIV*

"If you remain in me and my words remain in you, ask whatever you wish, and it will be done for you."
John 15:7 NIV

"No weapon formed against **YOU** *shall prosper, And every tongue which rises agains* **YOU** *in judgment you shall condemn. This is the heritage of the servants of the Lord, And their righteousness is from* **ME,"**

Memory 1

"We demolish arguments and every pretension that sets itself up against the knowledge of God, and we take captive every thought to make it obedient to Christ." 2 Corinthians 10:5 NIV

What are we thinking??? My Word for this year is **OBEDIENCE** and this scripture hits home for me....it's not only what I'm doing to obey Christ but it is also my thinking that needs to follow into obedience as well. I remember when God spoke to me to go and visit a friend of mine who wasn't a Christian. I kept arguing with God and said I didn't have enough time that day but I would go another day when I had a little more time. Well I never got the opportunity to ever visit that friend again. A week later she was killed in a car accident. That was a day I've lived to regret and I made a promise to myself and God, that day I got the news, that I would **Always Listen** and be **Obedient** to what He **Asks**. How do you go on when something like that happens in your life? You ask the Lord to forgive you, forgive yourself and cry many tears. Wow has this been a heart and eye opener for me today. I pray that it will be for you today as well. This is definitely one of those scriptures to HIDE in our HEARTS!

TAKE TIME TO PRAY:

Ask God what your mind is thinking that needs to follow under the **Obedience** of Christ. Think About this....What is Your **Word** that God is giving to you?

CHALLENGE:

What is God speaking to you about **Obedience**? Write your thoughts down below and MEMORIZE *2 Corinthians 10:5 NIV*

_____

_____

_____

_____

_____

_____

_____

_____

_____

_____

_____

_____

Memory 2

20. *"Now to him who is able to do immeasurably more than all we ask or imagine, according to his power that is at work within us,* **21.** *to him be glory in the church and in Christ Jesus throughout all generations for ever and ever! Amen." Ephesians 3:20-21 NIV*

How many times do we put limits on God? I know I have done that many times. This scripture is just popping out at me today. The first part states that Him "meaning God" is able to do more than we Ask or Imagine but the KEY is in the second part of Verse 20...."according to his **POWER** that is a work within us.... My husband and I were sending our kids to Christian School and one month we were short the money to pay for it. We didn't know where the money was going to come from and we prayed and asked God for his help. We were at church the night before the school fees were due and someone came up to us and said God had told them that we needed some money. We shared with them the story and they wrote a check right then and gave it to us. Whoa! Are we truly letting God's power transform us, flowing through our veins and spilling out on all of those around us? God is Able.... but are we willing to Ask and Believe? Today is the first day to transforming our hearts and minds allowing the Lord's power to work through us and in us.

TAKE TIME TO PRAY:

Lord, I am asking you today to allow the **POWER** of God to work in my Heart, Mind, Body and Spirit. Nothing is impossible with You. Help me to be an extension of You today and always.

CHALLENGE:

What is God speaking to you? Write your thoughts down below and MEMORIZE *Ephesians 3:20-21 NIV*

_____

_____

_____

_____

_____

_____

_____

_____

_____

_____

_____

_____

Memory 3

"If you remain in me and my words remain in you, ask whatever you wish, and it will be done for you."
John 15:7 NIV

I encourage you to read the whole Chapter of John 15. It's the story of Jesus talking about the vine and branches. I grew up in the Central Valley with vineyards all around me. My parents and I in the summers, during high school, would go out and glean vineyards after the harvesters for our cousin. We would pick the grapes that they missed on the vines. I learned a lot during that time and it was a lot of hard work but my parents were there working right beside me. Jesus is right beside us every day, just like my parents working with me in the grape vineyards. This brings us back to this scripture today, He wants our lives to be an example to everyone we meet, through our actions, the words we speak, we need to be a light to those around us. Ask Him to speak through you today. An added benefit with this scripture…it comes with a PROMISE! Ending today's "*Memory*" with this scripture.

"May these words of my mouth and this mediation of my heart be pleasing in your sight Lord, my Rock and my Redeemer." Psalms 19:14 NIV

TAKE TIME TO PRAY:

Lord I am so thankful for having wonderful parents who were always there for me. If you didn't have parents like mine, ask God to be your Father, your Mother....whoever you need Him to be for you today. Our Father is just waiting to lavish you with wonderful things He has in store for you as you draw closer to Him.

CHALLENGE:

Ask God to give you a memory when He has shown up in your life. Write your thoughts down below and MEMORIZE the scriptures above!

_____

_____

_____

_____

_____

_____

_____

_____

_____

_____

Memory 4

"Salvation is found in no one else, for there is no other name under heaven given to mankind by which we must be saved." Acts 4:12 NIV

The name JESUS....have you ever thought how much power there is in His name. When my husband was in the middle of cancer treatments, my girlfriend "Jacquelin" called me and said "Jerilyn, you just need to say the name "Jesus" when you pray for him. You know sometimes we think we need a long prayer telling Him everything in detail but in actuality, we don't. I cannot describe the peace that I felt through obediently praying the name "Jesus, Jesus, Jesus", gave to me. No other name can save, heal or give you peace. So no matter what you are going thru today, He knows. Just call His name, He's already there; right beside you.

TAKE TIME TO PRAY:

If you have never asked Jesus into your heart, there is no better time than now, if you've felt astranged from Him for awhile, call out the name of "Jesus" and see what happens. There is no other name that will calm the storm in your life.

CHALLENGE:

Write your thoughts down below and MEMORIZE these scriptures!

> *"The Lord himself goes before you and will be with you; he will never leave you nor forsake you. Do not be afraid; do not be discouraged." Deuteronomy 31:8 NIV*
> *"One who has unreliable friends soon comes to ruin, but there is a friend who sticks closer than a brother." Proverbs. 18:24 NIV*

_____

_____

_____

_____

_____

_____

_____

Memory 5

"Commit to the Lord whatever you do, and He will establish your plans." Proverbs 16:3 NIV

There is more power in this scripture than our minds can even fathom. Picture yourself every morning waking up and saying "Here's my day Lord, I'm giving it all to you". "I want you to take my life today and make it yours." "Help me to have a listening ear and an attentive heart to you today." "Work through me as an extension of you today." What would happen if we relinquished our lives to his control 24/7? There are times when he might tell us, *"Be still and know that I am God".* Psalms 46:10a NIV and then other times He might be saying this to us *"Learn to do right; seek justice. Defend the oppressed. Take up the cause of the fatherless; plead the case of the widow." Isaiah 1:17* NIV Whatever He is doing in your life today, the most important thing you can do is get on your knees and lay your day at the "FEET" of Jesus. You will not regret it.

(Memory about laying everything at the feet of Jesus) See "Memory Reference" at the back of book

TAKE TIME TO PRAY:

Lord help me give every day to you, from the morning when I rise until my head hits the pillow at night. May I see my life the way you see me Today and Always.

CHALLENGE:

Write your thoughts down below and MEMORIZE one of these scriptures!

"Commit to the lord whatever you do, and he will establish your plans." Proverbs 16:3 NIV
"Be still and know that I am God". Psalms 46:10a,
"Learn to do right; seek justice. Defend the oppressed. Take up the cause of the fatherless; plead the case of the widow." Isaiah 1:17 NIV

_____

_____

_____

_____

_____

_____

_____

Memory 6

"Blesssed is the one who does not walk in the step with the wicked or stand in the way that sinners take or sit in the company of mockers, 2.but whose delight in the law of the Lord, and who meditates on his law day and night. 3.That person is like a tree planted by streams of water which yields its fruit in season and whose leaf does not wither..... whatever they do prospers. Psalms 1:1-3 NIV

This scripture comes full circle for me and my life today. My hope is that it will do the same for you as well. This is one of the scriptures that my Sunday School Teacher had me memorize as a young child. The WHOLE Chapter....Psalms 1. Read it. The Word of God changes us, it changes the way we think....not like the world thinks. The worlds values change on a daily basis......"What's popular NOW", or should I say "What's Trending" NOW. Who are we FOLLOWING? The bible is full of guidelines for our lives and they are just as relevant NOW as they were when they were written. It is the only book that I've read, and then a week, a month or even a year later read the same verse and it resonated something totally different for me. This brings me back to my word "**Obedience**". Being in God's Word everyday, whether it's a whole chapter, single scripture, or memorizing a verse. From the busy mom, who feels like she doesn't have time or the busy executive running to the next meeting....Make Time. We all make time for the things that are most important to us and why wouldn't we do this if we really understood that it would be the SINGLE, most important, life changing decision we can make. Make this a Daily Habit, a Trend, a Share, a Post but most importantly....sinking your roots down deep into the Word will allow you to GROW into the Person that God Made you to be. Look at the last part of VERSE 3. As a "BUSY" person wanting to use my time wisely..."*whatever they do prospers*". I want to know that what I'm spending my time and energy on is not wasted.

TAKE TIME TO PRAY:

Lord, create in me the Habit and Desire to be in Your Word everyday and give me a vision, from this day forward, how different my life will be when I spend time and pray by being Obedient to you.

CHALLENGE:

Write your thoughts down below and MEMORIZE one of these scriptures in Psalms 1:1, 2 or 3 OR if you feel like really challenging yourself, Memorize the Whole chapter.

_____

_____

_____

_____

_____

_____

_____

_____

_____

_____

_____

_____

Memory 7

"A Generous Person will prosper; whoever refreshes others will be refreshed." Proverbs 11:25 NIV

I don't know if you can say anyone is born being generous. As a baby we couldn't have survived if our parents hadn't fed and nurtured us through all of the stages of life. Somewhere along the way, we started standing apart in our characteristics. I heard my Pastor speak in one of his sermons that a parent is their child's conscience. That's where we are taught right from wrong, how to make our bed, brush our teeth, go to church, pray and the list goes on and on. We all know that kids learn more by watching than by being told what to do....There is something to be said about visual learning! "Do as I say, not as I do, right? What kind of example are you setting to those around you that sets the scripture above into action. I watched my mom and dad growing up, great examples of servanthood, always lending a helping hand when needed. My mom made peach and apple pies, placing them in the freezer in case someone needed a meal. When the time came to serve, she was ready, willing and able, cooking the pie and sending it on its way with a wonderful homemade meal to go with it. I can almost smell the aroma in the kitchen of the pie baking now. In the day and age we live in, we call door dash and have food delivered to a friend. Don't misunderstand me, there is nothing wrong with that type of giving either but there is definitely something to be said about the time you spend doing the giving that helps to stir up and revive that generous spirit....Especially if it has been asleep for a while. I wonder who God is going to place in your path to Refresh Today. I hope you recognize it, act on it and be refreshed yourself.

TAKE TIME TO PRAY:

Lord, help me today to be generous and refresh others, as I act out of obedience to you, Refresh me as well.

CHALLENGE:

Write your thoughts down below and MEMORIZE one of these scriptures.

> *"In everything I did, I showed you that by this kind of hard work we must help the weak, remembering the words the Lord Jesus himself said: It is more blessed to give than to receive". Acts 20:35 NIV*

_____

_____

_____

_____

_____

_____

_____

_____

Memory 8

*"Come to me, all you who are weary and burdened, and I will give you rest. **29.** Take my yoke upon you and learn from me, for I am gentle and humble in heart, and you will find rest for your souls. **30.** For my yoke is easy and my burden is light". Matthew 11:28-30 NIV*

Have you ever found yourself in a situation where you are so busy you just don't know how you are going to get everything done. Even if you could get everything done, you don't have the energy to do it. I seem to find myself in this situation quite a bit and I am sure there are many of you reading this that can relate to the words that I am speaking. Maybe your heart is heavy because you've lost someone you love, maybe you've lost your job or you had a disagreement with someone you work with. Or you have found yourself procrastinating on continuing education that is required for your job or you have just recooperated from an illness and everything seems extremely overwhelming....even just getting out of bed. The Lord knows just how we feel. He tells us in the scripture above to "come to him, if you are weary and burdened and he will give you rest"....we will find rest for our souls. Sometimes it is not just our physical bodies that need rest but our **SOUL** and **SPIRIT** that needs rest. It's amazing when our Soul and Spirit are allowed rest how it affects our body. It's times like these that I close my eyes and picture myself being held in the arms of Jesus. Just the mental picture of that in my mind gives me such a peace that I can't even describe it to you. Try doing the same and see what happens to you.

TAKE TIME TO PRAY:

Lord, I come to you today with a heavy heart and I cast all of the worries of this life on your shoulders. I need to rest in the arms of You (Jesus) today.

CHALLENGE:

Write your thoughts down below and MEMORIZE Matthew 11:28-30. There will come a day when you really need it and you will be able to pull it out of your Memory Bank, your wonderful mind He created in you.

_____

_____

_____

_____

_____

_____

_____

_____

_____

_____

_____

Memory 9

"If you, then, though you are evil, know how to give good gifts to your children, how much more will your Father in heaven give good gifts to those who ask Him!" Matthew 7:11 NIV

My dad is no longer here with me on earth but has gone to be with Jesus. But when my dad was here, he was always listening to everything I said, thinking of ways he could bless me. If I told him there was something that I needed, the next thing I knew he was trying to do everything in his power to get that for me. I remember one time when I was planning a Winnie the Pooh Birthday party for my daughter and I wanted a sign to stick in the lawn. He asked me if I had a picture of the sign and I showed him the one that I had found in her Winnie the Pooh book. The next week I was over visiting my parents and he took me out in his workshop and there was the sign, exactly like the picture in the book. I feel very blessed to have had a super talented dad that was so giving and generous. If our earthly Dad's want to give us good gifts, how much more does our heavenly Father want to give us gifts as well. There is one simple thing that we sometimes forget to do and that is ASK! It's just a small 3 letter word which carries a whole lot of Power. So next time you are in need of something, go to your Heavenly Father first. He wants to meet those needs in our lives every day but sometimes we just plain forget to ASK!

"If you believe, you will receive whatever you ask for in prayer." Matthew. 21:22 NIV

TAKE TIME TO PRAY:

Lord, You say in your word that you want to give good gifts to your children, if we ask. You also tell us in your word that if we believe, we will receive whatever we ask for in prayer. I come to you today, asking you to answer my prayers, not from a selfish heart, but a heart full of desire to please you and find your favor in my life.

CHALLENGE:

Write your thoughts down below and MEMORIZE one of the scriptures above. You will be amazed what God will do in your life as you start memorizing and allowing the scriptures to sink down deep in your heart, mind and soul.

_____

_____

_____

_____

_____

_____

_____

_____

_____

_____

Memory 10

*"If any of you lacks wisdom, you should ask God,
who gives generously to all without finding fault,
and it will be given to you." James 1:5 NIV*
*"The fear of the Lord is the beginning of knowledge,
but fools despise wisdom and instruction." Prov. 1:7*

A few years ago, I did a women's bible study on the Book of James. So much is packed in those 5 chapters. Wisdom, perseverance, good and perfect gifts, temptation, being a doer of the word, listening, freedom, religious spirit and that is just in the first Chapter of James. Whew!!!! I would encourage you to read the entire chapter of James. The Bible study instructed us every week to read the ENTIRE Book of James. I will tell you what that did for me....it soaked into my spirit. Wisdom is the Scripture that I chose to share on today. *"If any of you lacks wisdom, you should ask God, who gives generously to all without finding fault, and it will be given to you."* It's not conditional, He doesn't look for fault, He doesn't even say you have to be a Christian, it is written that you just have to ASK....there's that powerful word again......"And it will be given to you." I know I sometimes overthink things but Jesus tells us many things throughout His Word in just a few simple words. ASK, SEEK, BE STILL, FAITH and last but not least WISDOM!!!!! Start by repeating the 1st verse in James 1:5 *"If any of you lacks wisdom, you should ask God, who gives generously to all without finding fault, and it will be given to you."* and then end by repeating the verse in Proverbs 1:7 *"The fear of the Lord is the beginning of knowledge, but fools despise wisdom and instruction."* Write your thoughts down below and in the weeks to come watch how this one word "Wisdom" and just by "Asking" for it, changes everything you do from this day forward.

TAKE TIME TO PRAY:

Lord, if I lack wisdom, Your Word says that all I have to do is ask of You and You will freely give it to me without any conditions. I want to seek your wisdom today in everything that I do, every person that I meet and every decision that I make today and from this day forward. I Thank You Lord for hearing and answering my prayers.

CHALLENGE:

Write your thoughts down below and MEMORIZE one of the scriptures above. God will meet you where you are and may His Wisdom that comes from Him, be the driving force of your life.

_____

_____

_____

_____

_____

_____

_____

_____

_____

_____

_____

Memory 11

"What good is it, my brothers and sisters, if someone claims to have faith but has no deeds. Can such faith save them?" James 2:14 NIV "In the same way, faith by itself, if it is not accompanied by action, is dead." James 2:17 NIV "As the Body without the spirit is dead, so Faith without deeds is dead." James 2:26 NIV

Faith is what I call a "One Liner". It comes with a Punch. Faith...God's word says, Without *Faith* it is impossible to please him, *Faith* comes by hearing and hearing by the word of God, *Faith* is the substance of things hoped for but the evidence of things not seen, For it is by Grace that you have been saved, through *Faith*.....The NIV version has mentioned the word "FAITH" 254 times in the bible. *Faith* is a word that is accompanied by action. We do a lot of things in our lives not even realizing it took Faith to do it. Like when you get in your car to go to work and have *"Faith"* that the car is going to start. That can seem very inconsequential but if it didn't start you wouldn't have a way to get to work. We get up knowing that the lights are going to turn on or water is going to run out of the faucet so we can take a shower or brush our teeth. These things can be frustrating if they're not working but the real test of our *Faith* is when we hear someone has an incurable disease, or a friend, a child, a spouse or a parent dies unexpectedly. This is when true *Faith* has to rise to the occasion and is tested. The question is "Do we really trust him"? How could a God who loves us so much take away someone we love so deeply? Do we have the *Faith* to believe that the Lord always knows best? I don't have the answers to these questions but one thing I do know is that I have put my life in God's hands, knowing that he can take care of me far better than I can take care of myself. This is the one thing that I will have the *Faith* to believe. Unfortunately we will never be protected from bad things happening to us but we can have the *Faith* and assurance knowing what God's word tells us *"And we know that in all things God works for the Good of those who love him, who have been called according to his purpose."* *Romans 8:28 NIV*

TAKE TIME TO PRAY:

Lord, where I lack Faith in my life fill me up, help me always to believe that You know best no matter the circumstances.

CHALLENGE:

Write your thoughts down below, maybe there is something that hit home in your heart today that you're struggling with, let him know, he already knows anyway and MEMORIZE one of these scriptures. God give me Faith to believe Today and Always!

_____

_____

_____

_____

_____

_____

_____

_____

_____

_____

_____

Memory 12

"Be joyful in hope, patient in affliction, faithful in prayer. Share with the Lord's people who are in need. Practice hospitality." Romans 12: 12-13 NIV

I was in charge of the funeral dinners at our church for a few years and it was a definite commitment, but what a Joy it was to serve. I used this scripture as a theme for all we did, it goes along with this Scripture....it's better to give than to receive.... I had a wonderful group of ladies who would help and serve with me whenever I called them. There were many families that we served over the years that didn't understand why we did this. When people are going through mourning, their hearts are very sensitive and open to the Holy Spirit...this is a time, like no other, when we can truly minister to people and their needs. Many times we prayed with them right there in the church kitchen. We may never know the impact we had on their lives until we get to heaven. The word in Romans 12:15-16 NIV tells us *"Rejoice with those who rejoice; mourn with those who mourn. Live in harmony with one another. Do not be proud, but be willing to associate with people of low position. Do not be conceited."* This speaks to the very bottom of my heart. I am so guilty of acting like this, thinking better of myself than others, Lord please forgive me for ever feeling this way. Now, when I hear of a need, I have a deep desire to be obedient to God's Word. Is it a sacrifice? At times it can be, but greater is the reward and a deeper peace than you can imagine when you are obedient to what God is calling you to do. Have you had that quiet and gentle whisper, say.... Go to your neighbor and take them some cookies, invite them to church, take them a meal or offer to mow their lawn.

Listening to that gentle whisper might seem a little odd the first couple of times you act on it, but I guarantee you can never go wrong when you are doing what the Lord has asked you to do. Your spirit will SOAR!!!!!!!!!!!!!!!!!!!

TAKE TIME TO PRAY:

Lord, help me today to listen to your gentle and quiet whisper and follow You in obedience. Following you and being obedient is the key to great rewards in my life.

CHALLENGE:

Give your thoughts a chance to form below, maybe you have been struggling with some of the things that were written down in today's memory. Memorize one of these scriptures. Hide them deep in your heart and ask God what he wants to change!

_____

_____

_____

_____

_____

_____

_____

_____

_____

_____

_____

_____

Memory 13

"Therefore do not be foolish, but understand what the Lord's will is." Ephesians 5:17 NIV

Do any of us really know what God's will is for our life? God says he will order our Steps. My husband and I have always believed that God would Open a Door and we just had to use wisdom and recognize that it was him opening the door. We also made an agreement that if the door was opened we would walk through it. This kind of obedience to Christ has been the biggest blessing in our lives….this started for us from the time we bought our first home and God provided a home that we picked up on public auction, when my dad passed away and we needed to find a home that had Mother-in-law quarters so my mom could live with us, God provided it. It had been on the market for 2 years. By doing an exchange on an investment property, we were able to purchase a vacation home, a wonderful retreat to share with others. We sold a home we had lived in for 20 years, in a time when not a lot of properties were selling and then the house that we found wasn't even on the market. This is just a small part of a larger picture on how we began to see God's will open and close doors at the right time in our lives; if you listen, obey and use wisdom. In one of the memories ahead, I will share how God has healed and protected my family, carrying us thru everything that we've had to face. Wisdom and Obedience go hand in hand.

"For through wisdom your days will be many, and years will be added to your life." Proverbs 9:11 NIV
"For I know the plans I have for you declares the Lord, plans to prosper you and not to harm you, plans to give you a hope and a future." Jeremiah 29:11 NIV

TAKE TIME TO PRAY:

Lord, I want my steps to be ordered by you and I want you to guide me all through my life. Help me to Walk thru every door that you Open and recognize the doors that I am to walk through.

CHALLENGE:

Take the time to melt these scriptures over your heart, sinking in the aroma of Christ. Ask God to show you his path for your life. MEMORIZE a scripture for wisdom and his promise of years to be added to your life!

_____

_____

_____

_____

_____

_____

_____

_____

_____

_____

_____

Memory 14

"Therefore confess your sins to each other and pray for each other so that you may be healed. The prayer of a righteous person is powerful and effective." James 5:16 NIV

After my mom passed away, it left a big whole in my life. She had lived with our family for 14 years, when I wanted to talk, ask someone for help, or needed someone to pray with me for a specific need, my mom was always there, ready, willing and able. You know how the saying goes, "you never know what you had until it's gone", that is exactly how I felt. It filled me with Joy knowing someone was praying with me and for me. That was taken from me when my mom went to be with Jesus. I was talking to a friend on the phone one day and was sharing with her how I felt and she said "I can be your prayer partner!" That was 8 years ago and those 6 words changed my life. In the months that followed we added a few more ladies and now there are 4 of us that we call "Prayer Warriors". We live all over the United States now but have a common bond. Our families attended a Spirit Filled church together at in a small town in Central California. We have laughed together, cried together, prayed together and seen God perform many miracles in the people we've prayed for as well as our own lives and our families lives. I have the answered prayers written down in my prayer journal. They are under my "THANKFUL" List. I've said many times I want the devil to know that "when my feet hit the floor, the devil says oh crap she's up". Since then I've started another group with 4-5 women that know how to pray as well and I share a scripture and a meaning almost every day thru text. We also pray for needs of others and our own. Technology has been a great avenue for sharing with each other. If I may encourage you to step out and start a prayer texting group. A thought may come, "I Don't have time", you will always have time to do the most important things in your Life.....Prayer needs to be "Top on your List". Be all God wants you to be Today. ...."*The prayer of a righteous person is powerful and effective.*"

TAKE TIME TO PRAY:

Lord, I want to be an effective prayer warrior for you and I know you hear and answer my prayers. Give me faith to believe, the discipline to do what you have called me to do and the strength to see your will accomplished through me. Amen!

CHALLENGE:

God wants you to be a Prayer Warrior and by MEMORIZING this scripture and the others you have been daily working on, you will be..Growing everyday with him. Write it below.

_____

_____

_____

_____

_____

_____

_____

_____

_____

_____

Memory 15

"Lord my God, I called to you for help, and you healed me." Psalms 30:2 NIV

WOW, this is a memory that is a little hard to explain because I don't know how you believe but I am going to put myself out there and share my story. I feel like this has happened to me to share with you...for such a time is this. Definitely Faith Building so here it goes! I was at choir rehearsal before Sunday morning service, and my jaws felt like they were on fire. I continued to sing and then I heard this quiet whisper, telling me that surgery was being performed on my jaws. (You probably need to know the back story of why my jaws needed healing, right? I had my wisdom teeth extracted and when they did the surgery, they hyperextended my jaws. It caused my jaws to pop loudly every time I chewed. Then after time went on, they began to lock shut. I'd get out of bed every morning with my jaws locked and within about 30 minutes after getting up, they would unlock. Well one morning they didn't unlock. My jaws stayed locked for about a year.) Now to continue the Healing Story....Over this time I prayed and asked for healing and it didn't come, I didn't know why but one thing I've learned about prayer and answered prayer, is that God has a specific time for everything. He also wants to know that we don't give up and like the parable In the bible about the woman going before the judge again and again, I think he just says "Ok I'll answer your prayers", right? As I heard the quiet whisper... with my jaws feeling like they were on fire, the tears started rolling down my cheeks. I remembered my daughter-in-law having surgery and they had to break her jaw to correct her bite. Her jaws were wired shut for weeks. The Lord"s quiet whisper again saying this is the way the healing was happening in my jaws. Over the next weeks when I was singing in choir, I began to share my story of healing with the choir members and every week my jaws would open a little wider and a little wider until finally, after about 6 weeks, I could totally open my jaws. My jaws have not locked since that time. No matter how small or how big our miracles are, they are still miracles. When you've experienced divine healing for yourself, it grows your faith, your ears tune in to the holy spirit speaking to you and you begin to listen and stay tuned in. If God can do this for me, who am I, he will certainly do this for you....Ask, Believe & Receive!

TAKE TIME TO PRAY:

I want to be the person that never gives up praying and I will perservere in my prayers until you answer, Yes, No, Maybe or Not Now.

CHALLENGE:

Memorize the Scripture above, this is an easy one liner but it is so powerful. Write any thoughts down below that come to your mind.

_____

_____

_____

_____

_____

_____

_____

_____

_____

_____

_____

Memory 16

*"The Lord makes firm the steps of the one who delights in him; **24** though he may stumble, he will not fall, for the Lord upholds him with his hand." Psalm 37:23-24 NIV*

6. *"Do not be anxious about anything, but in every situation, by prayer and petition, with thanksgiving, present your requests to God. **7.** And the Peace of God, which transcends all understanding, will guard your hearts and your minds in Christ Jesus." Philippians 4:6-7 NIV*

In Memory 13, I said would go into more details how God has healed and protected our family, carrying us through everything that we've had to face. It is very true that Wisdom and Obedience go hand in hand. It started out about 6 years ago when we were woken up by the police at about midnight. Our daughter had been in a bad car accident. A horse ran in front of her car and the windshield had been crushed into the left side of her face and eye as the horse rolled over her car. That is one phone call, as a parent, you never want to get. It was traumatizing for everyone and my heart just hurt for my daughter. Miraculously, she had no broken bones, the skin around her eye had been cut from the glass but there was not a single piece of glass found in her eye and she had a large scrape on the side of her face. Praise the Lord! Yes, it was hard for her and us too, but when you think of what could have happened! I know beyond a shadow of a doubt God was protecting her that night from further injury. The above scripture in Psalm 37:23-24 rings true in my life, The Lord makes firm our steps if we delight in him, we may stumble but we won't fall and the Lord·holds us in his hands. I've never felt such an overwhelming peace as I did that night and in the months to come, guarding our hearts and minds through Christ. You are probably wondering how she is doing today? It has been a long process and not trying to downplay it at all, it was not easy especially for her. She is a beautiful and smart young woman, inside and out, who knows how special she is to God and her Family. If you saw her today, you would never know that she went through an accident like this. We all learned how precious life is and to never take things for granted as well as telling people you love them before they walk out the door. Peace doesn't mean we won't have problems in our lives, peace is just the promise of the presence of God with us.

TAKE TIME TO PRAY:

God grant me Peace today in my life, in whatever circumstance that I am facing now. Guard my heart and my mind and make my steps firm as I delight in you.

CHALLENGE:

Memorize Scripture. You won't regret it and God help me not forget it.

_____

_____

_____

_____

_____

_____

_____

_____

_____

_____

_____

_____

Memory 17

"Do not conform to the pattern of this world, but be transformed by the renewing of your mind. Then you will be able to test and approve what God's will is..His good, pleasing and perfect will."
Romans 12:2 NIV

How many times have we asked God what his will is for our lives? I know for me it is at the forefront of my mind every day. I want to share this one day in particular that still blows me away every time I think about it. My husband had been working as a loan officer and I had my own business at the time. 3 small children and as most of you know with a young family, there are always a lot of expenses. Before my husband took this job we had prayed and felt God leading him in this direction. All of the doors opened for him to walk through and everything was going great until one day he came home and shared what had happened that day at work. The company had been sold and the new owners were doing things that just didn't line up with our beliefs and staying true to who we are. When he told me this, I felt like "a deer in the headlights" I went to my prayer room and cried out to God, "why Lord is this happening, we prayed about the direction that you wanted us to go and you led us here". "You opened every door for us to walk through and we were obedient and walked thru it." "Why, Why, Why?" As I was sitting their crying I heard that quiet whisper speak to me. "Yes, you were obedient and were in my will, but sometimes other people make wrong decisions and choices that affect your lives. This is where you need to seek me again for my will to be done." This awakened something in my Spirit. I had to repeat this as

I prayed "So Lord you are telling me we were in your will and because someone else made a wrong choice that affected our decisions, we have to go a different direction?" "Ok Lord, I get it." The scripture above tells it like it is, don't conform to what the world standards are. Let God transform your mind and by doing this you will be able to test and approve His perfect will. Ask Him and I guarantee He will tell you every time....through circumstances, doors that open or most importantly through His Word and prayer.

TAKE TIME TO PRAY:

Lord, I am asking you to show me the will you have for my life today and every day from here on out. Speak to me through your Holy Spirit and guide my steps.

CHALLENGE:

Memorize this Scripture. It will guide you through every twist and turn that you come to. Don't Forget...God has an Aerial View of Your Life. Write your thoughts down below.

_____

_____

_____

_____

_____

_____

_____

_____

_____

_____

_____

_____

Memory 18

"The way of fools seems right to them, but the wise listen to advice." Proverbs 12:15 NIV

My husband and I have always tried to lead by example. We've told our kids that when making a decision they should pray about it and ask the Lord for wisdom and seek wise counsel from others who use wisdom in making decisions. The scripture above tells us that the fools ways seem right but the wise listen to advice. Every decision that we've made in our marriage, has been a way of following under the obedience of Christ. We've looked at it as an opportunity to be in God's will and follow His Words. This allows you to see the direction you are to go and to also listen to the wise counsel of others who have gone through the same experiences. Maybe some people have made wrong choices and don't want you to follow down that same path. Sometimes they can be your parents, close friends or maybe even another family member. Making the right choice by listening to wise counsel (advice) and a second set of eyes and ears on your decision will guide you down the right path. Asking God for wisdom, praying, reading his word, and seeking wise counsel (advice) are the steps that we have followed in our lives. We've never listened to counsel from people that didn't make wise decisions. Our lives produce the fruit of who we are. If the lives of those we seek advice from aren't producing fruit, then they are not people we want to seek wise counsel from. Whether you are married or single, I hope after reading this, you will follow your heart and do the same.

"But Seek first his Kingdom and his righteousness, and all these things will be given to you as well." Matthew 6:33 NIV

****(Memory about God's confirmation of His Word..Seeking Wise Counsel) See " Memory Reference" section at the back of the book.***

TAKE TIME TO PRAY:

Lord guide me in every decision that I make. I'm asking you for wisdom, by reading Your Word and seeking wise counsel.

CHALLENGE:

Memorize the scripture above. It is short and small but it is mighty. Here's another scripture to look at and memorize
"For the word of God is alive and active. Sharper than any doubled-edged sword, it penetrates even to dividing soul and spirit, joints and marrow; it judges the thoughts and attitudes of the heart."
Hebrews 4:12 NIV

_____

_____

_____

_____

_____

_____

_____

_____

Memory 19

"Blessed are the peacemakers for they will be called Children of God." Matthew 5:9 NIV

Our minds are so much like computers. They store up memories and remnants from the past. A smell, a place or a word spoken can bring it back to the forefront of your mind. This scripture was put into practice one day while I was working. I'm sure some of you can relate with a same situation at work or maybe even church or disagreement between co-workers. Maybe you were in the middle of it or you're the boss and you had to intervene in the situation. Well this is my story...I was an assistant at an accounting firm and my bosses were literally fighting on whose work I was going to do first. All of the sudden this scripture popped up in my mind, *"Blessed are the Peacemakers for they will be called Children of God."* "Whoa" I said to myself, "Where did that come from". I hadn't thought about that scripture in years...(I first memorized that scripture with my Sunday School teacher that had the suitcase full of treasures – "See Dedication Story"). What a Day...that scripture helped me to diffuse a situation, everyone was happy and the work was completed. Reflecting today as I am writing this, I've realized how vitally important it is to take time to MEMORIZE scripture. If you haven't had a situation like this in your life where God brings scriptures to the forefront of your mind, I can assure you, it **WILL** happen. You are never too OLD or too YOUNG to start memorizing. Start small and work your way up. Open your heart up to the Lord and ask him to Sharpen your mind for memorizing scripture...**YOU CAN DO IT!**

TAKE TIME TO PRAY:

Lord help me be alert and ready to hear your whispers of scriptures that I have read and memorized. Sharpen my mind to attach those scriptures to every cell in my brain. Sometimes it does not come easy for me but I know with your help, I can do all things.

CHALLENGE:

Memorize this Scripture above about being a Peacemaker. It is short and small, but it will come to your rescue when you need it. And when you are doubting yourself, here's another one....

> "I can do all things through Christ who strengthens me." Philippians 4:13 NKJV

_____

_____

_____

_____

_____

_____

_____

_____

_____

Memory 20

"For God has not given us a spirit of fear, but of power and of love and of a sound mind." 2 Timothy 1:7 NKJV

FEAR...How many of you have ever been afraid? I know I have many times in my life. We can either let **FEAR** control our lives or we can let **FEAR** drive us in a different direction. I know some of us have had things happen in our lives that make us fearful because of that memory. Before my husband and I got married he was coming to my parents house, he was late and didn't call and then the phone call came that he had been in a bad car accident. For years, I had that fear come over me everytime he was late or the call didn't come. I'm sure if you have gone through fear like this, you know what I am talking about. Some things are probably coming to mind and the anxiety that comes from that fear is driven by that memory. Our memories trigger a lot of responses in the brain and when we fill it up with God's word it is a counter attack for our fear and anxiety. The bible says in *John 10:10 NKJV "The thief does not come except to steal, and to kill, and to destroy. I have come that they may have life, and that they may have it more abundantly."* This is the 20th day MEMORY and I hope YOU all know by now this devotion is all about MEMORIZING the Bible. *Ephesians 6:17 NIV says "Take the helmet of salvation and the sword of the Spirit, which is the word of God."* God's word is a weapon we have to attack **FEAR** head on and if we have read the Word and memorized it, it will be our Sword. Here is an acronym that I love about **FEAR**. This is just one of many that I have used when needed as a reminder of what is real. It directs me back to "Pick

Up my Sword". I'm not sure where I heard it but it has glued itself to my brain. **FEAR ......** **F** alse **E** vidence **A** ppearing **R** eal. So when you become fearful remember this acronmyn but more importantly remember 2 Timothy 1:7.

TAKE TIME TO PRAY:

Oh Lord, You are my Father, my protector and my shield. Your Word is my Sword and Conqueror over fear. May that be my first thought and not my last when I become afraid. Show me the areas in my life that I am fearful and need to surrender to You.

CHALLENGE:

Memorize this Scripture on **Fear**. This is also a good one to memorize.

> *"For our struggle is not against flesh and blood, but against the rulers, against the authorities, against the powers of this dark world and against the spiritual forces of evil in the heavenly realms."*
> *Ephesians 6:12 NIV*

_____

_____

_____

_____

_____

_____

_____

_____

Memory 21

"For we are God's handiwork, created in Christ Jesus to do good works, which God's prepared in advance for us to do." Ephesians 2:10 NIV

How many of you have ever had a **Dream**? A **Dream** can be a wish or desire. **Dreams** can be just a thought. A **Dream** can also be images or stories created in your brain while you're sleeping. Does anything come to your mind? Then there comes that word doubt, "that will never happen". When we put our life in God's hands, he will lead us in the direction he wants us to go but it's up to us to walk through the doors or windows that he opens. Sit back and think how your choices and decisions have led you to where you are now....Our choices and decisions are all building blocks that just stack one on top of the other. If we make a wrong decision along the way it can make our foundation weak and it will crumble and fall. That's were we have to start all over again. A few years ago my husband and I decided together to read Rick Warren's book, "The Purpose Driven Life" – "What on Earth am I Here For". We started reading the book before Easter. I had read the book several times but I had not read it with my husband. We have read books together in joint bible studies but this was different. I think we grew more in that reading than we ever had before. The Book is full of scripture and application for applying the word to your life. This book planted a seed in my husband's life to start sending out devotions to our children everyday. It birthed in me a deeper desire to be in God's word and the need for a prayer time everyday. And here we are today on the last day of this Memory and devotional, a dream, a desire and seeds that were planted by many people in my life over the years. If I have learned anything in life up to this point, it's that God needs to be my first priority, family second and everything else will fall into place.. This next scripture completes this Memory for Today. *"Now to him who is able to do immeasurably more than all we ask or imagine, according to his power that is at work within us." Ephesians 3:20.* NIV If we don't allow God to work in our lives, it will never happen. It's all up to US!

TAKE TIME TO PRAY:

Father don't allow me to give up on my **Dreams**. Help me to follow the plan you have for my life and guide each of my steps in the right direction. Work in my life today and always.

CHALLENGE:

Memorize this scripture above and write down anything that God is speaking to you today. God's power is in us, we just need to exercise it to make us Strong!

_____

_____

_____

_____

_____

_____

_____

_____

_____

_____

Memory References

"Lay everything at the Feet of Jesus when you Pray": Memory 5

Usually the best time for me to pray for people is when God wakes me up in the middle of the night. My own joke behind this is that's the only time I'm still enough that he can get my attention. One night I woke up and the Lord was urging me to get up and pray. I didn't know why and I didn't want to wake up my husband so I very quietly went and knelt down by a Chaise that we had in our bedroom and started praying. Before long, still not knowing why I was praying, I heard the Lord's quiet whisper telling me to lay prostrate on the ground, so I did. I don't remember how long I laid there.....probably around 20 minutes, then I got up and went back to bed and fell asleep. The next night was church and our Pastor was speaking about Abraham and how Abraham would lay prostrate before the Lord because that's where the blessings of God are. All of the sudden tears filled my eyes and I saw a picture, in my mind, of myself praying the night before....praying prostrate on the ground at Jesus's feet. That is a picture that is forever etched in my mind. So when God tells me to get up and pray, I GET UP AND PRAY!

*** "God's Confirmation of his Word...Seeking Wise Counsel" Chapter, Isaiah 58: Memory 18***

My husband and I went to a church that we had attended since our kids were young and now they'd grown up. We were trying to find our way and what our purpose was in serving in the church, so we called our friends who were ministers in another state. We expressed to them what we were feeling and he started speaking divine words of wisdom. He said "you guys need to get a pen and paper and write this down, the Lord wants you to remember this". So I began writing as he told us that God was going to use us in a mighty way and we would be called the **"Repairer of the Breach".** Those words really struck a cord within me. I'd never heard that phrase before and I wasn't sure what it meant or where it was coming from, but knew we needed to be obedient to what God was telling us through our friends. By the time we got off the phone it was 11:00 p.m. and not even realizing it, we had been on the phone with them for 2 hours. They live in Arkansas and were 2 hours ahead of us. You really know who your friends are when they are willing to stay on the phone with you that long and that late. Note, this was a Thursday night. We went to church on Sunday, sitting in service and listening as our Pastor began reading Isaiah 58. As he was reading, my husband and I looked at each other wide eyed, and started pointing at the scripture that read *"And your ancient ruins shall be rebuilt; you shall raise up the foundations of many generations; you shall be called the **"Repairer of the Breach"**, the Restorer of streets to dwell in", Isaiah 58:12 Revised Standard.* I don't think my husband and I heard another word that was said. We were just in awe of the words that had been spoken by our friends and then our Pastor speaking on that very scripture this Sunday. How could we ever doubt that was God speaking through our friends and then our Pastor? Since that time,we have followed in obedience to do what God has specifically called us to do. God spoke to us through wise counsel and His Word which was confirmed to us when our Pastor delivered that sermon. Over the years, our friends have been there for us as we have been there for them. Talk about building your FAITH. I realize God sometimes shows up in small ways and sometimes in very BIG ways. Never doubt that God Speaks to You, whether it be through friends giving wise advise, his word or through prayer!

Family & Friends:

It takes 3 weeks to form a habit which is why there are 21 days of Memory devotions and a book full of verses. Also, its kind of Funny that I work for Century 21. I Hope you have enjoyed these "Numbered Memories" as I have shared and expressed my heart from my own life experiences....But more Importantly, that I've been able to Plants Seeds, Challenge and Inspire you to memorize scripture, be in God's Word and Pray everyday. God has been inspiring me even more as I have been obedient to his quiet whispers. Be on the Watch for **"Make a Memory Every Day" Vol. 2.**

About the Author

Jerilyn Pallesi Von Flue grew up in a small farming town in Central California. For the last 20 years she has been in the Real Estate business and 17 of those years has been working for Century 21 as a Manager/Realtor. She married her husband when she was 10 years old (LOL) and they have been married for 40 years. She is a mother of 3 children and 8 grandchildren. She's always smiling and her nickname is "Sunshine", given to her by an aunt when she was a teenager. An avid lover of reading, walk/running and leasurely bike rides, watching the moon rise in the sky, and traveling to new places. When she can't travel she loves Staycations. She also has a passion for COOKING which through "prayer prompting" led to a "Hot Momma's Cooking Clips" Facebook page. She felt is was truly a "God Moment" that she started March 2020, right before "Shelter In Place" happened. No matter the weather, she loves being able to enjoy the outdoors in rain or shine or even SNOW! Her sister, Diane, has another Nickname for her...."The Snow Queen". It's a joke between them, when visiting her in Idaho, she says "Everywhere YOU go, it SNOWS". When Jerilyn is asked what her biggest accomplishment in life is, she would tell you this, "Loving God, Family and All of her Wonderful Friends, and Praying for them Daily".